Buying A Foreclosed Home With Houses In Florida Real Estate

Find Homes For Sale In Florida &

Finance Houses For Sale In Florida

by

Brian Mahoney

Join Our VIP Mailing List and Get FREE Money Making Training Videos! Then Start Making Money within 24 hours!
Plus if you join our Mailing list you can get Revised and New Edition versions of your book free!

And Notifications of other FREE Offers!

Just Hit/Type in the Link Below

https://mahoneyproducts.wixsite.com/win1

FLORIDA REAL ESTATE

Get Our Video Training Program at:

**(Zero Cost Internet Marketing complete 142
video series)**

https://goo.gl/Qed1dY

http://www.BrianSMahoney.com

ABOUT THE AUTHOR

Brian Mahoney is the author of over 300 business start-up guides, real estate investing programs and Christian literature. He started his company MahoneyProducts in 1992.

He served in the US Army and worked over a decade for the US Postal Service. An active real estate investor, he has also served as a minister for the Churches of Christ in Virginia and Michigan.

He has degree's in Business Administration and Applied Science & Computer Programming.

His books and video training programs have helped thousands of people all over the world start there own successful business.

http://www.briansmahoney.com/

DEDICATION

**This book is dedicated to my son's
Matthew and Christian.
A blessing from God and the joy of my life.**

ACKNOWLEDGMENTS

I WOULD LIKE TO ACKNOWLEDGE ALL THE HARD WORK OF THE MEN AND WOMEN OF THE UNITED STATES MILITARY, WHO RISK THEIR LIVES ON A DAILY BASIS, TO MAKE THE WORLD A SAFER PLACE.

Disclaimer

This book was written as a guide to starting a business. As with any other high yielding action, starting a business has a certain degree of risk. This book is not meant to take the place of accounting, legal, financial or other professional advice. If advice is needed in any of these fields, you are advised to seek the services of a professional.

While the author has attempted to make the information in this book as accurate as possible, no guarantee is given as to the accuracy or currency of any individual item. Laws and procedures related to business are constantly changing.

Therefore, in no event shall Brian Mahoney, the author of this book be liable for any special, indirect, or consequential damages or any damages whatsoever in connection with the use of the information herein provided.

Table of Contents

FLORIDA REAL ESTATE

CHAPTER 1

ALL ABOUT FORECLOSURES

The Foreclosure Process

Foreclosure

Foreclosure is a legal process in which a lender attempts to recover the balance of a loan from a borrower, who has stopped making payments to the lender, by forcing the sale of the asset used as the collateral for the loan.

Formally, a mortgage lender (mortgagee), or other lienholder, obtains a termination of a mortgage borrower (mortgagor)'s equitable right of redemption, either by court order or by operation of law (after following a specific statutory procedure).

Usually a lender obtains a security interest from a borrower who mortgages or pledges an asset like a house to secure the loan. If the borrower defaults and the lender tries to repossess the property, courts of equity can grant the borrower the equitable right of redemption if the borrower repays the debt. While this equitable right exists, it is a cloud on title and the lender cannot be sure that they can repossess the property. Therefore, through the process of foreclosure, the lender seeks to foreclose (in plain English, immediately terminate) the equitable right of redemption and take both legal and equitable title to the property in fee simple. Other lien holders can also foreclose the owner's right of redemption for other debts, such as for overdue taxes, unpaid contractors' bills or overdue homeowners' association dues or assessments.

The foreclosure process as applied to residential mortgage loans is a bank or other secured creditor selling or repossessing a parcel of real property after the owner has failed to comply with an agreement between the lender and borrower called a "mortgage" or "deed of trust". Commonly, the violation of the mortgage is a default in payment of a promissory note, secured by a lien on the property. When the process is complete, the lender can sell the property and keep the proceeds to pay off its mortgage and any legal costs, and it is typically said that "the lender has foreclosed its mortgage or lien." If the promissory note was made with a recourse clause then if the sale does not bring enough to pay the existing balance of principal and fees the mortgagee can file a claim for a deficiency judgment. In many states in the United States, items included to calculate the amount of a deficiency judgment include the loan principal, accrued interest and attorney fees less the amount the lender bid at the foreclosure sale.

Types of Foreclosure

The mortgage holder can usually initiate foreclosure at a time specified in the mortgage documents, typically some period of time after a default condition occurs. Within the United States, Canada and many other countries, several types of foreclosure exist. In the U.S., two of them – namely, by judicial sale and by power of sale – are widely used, but other modes of foreclosure are also possible in a few states.

Judicial Foreclosure

judicial foreclosure. n. a judgment by a court in favor of foreclosure of a mortgage or deed of trust, which orders that the real property which secured the debt be sold under foreclosure proceedings to pay the debt.

Nonjudicial Foreclosure

When you take out a loan in a state that primarily uses a nonjudicial foreclosure process, you sign a deed of trust or mortgage that typically contains a power of sale clause. If you have a power of sale provision in your mortgage contract, the lender can foreclose without going to court.

Strict Foreclosure

Strict foreclosure refers to foreclosure of a mortgage without a sale of the mortgaged property, being accomplished by a suit in equity and a decree rendered therein. It extinguishes the mortgagor's equity of redemption.

Acceleration

A contract provision that allows a lender to require a borrower to repay all or part of an outstanding loan if certain requirements are not met. An acceleration clause outlines the reasons that the lender can demand loan repayment. Also known as "acceleration covenant".

Process

The process of foreclosure can be rapid or lengthy and varies from state to state. Other options such as refinancing, a short sale, alternate financing, temporary arrangements with the lender, or even bankruptcy may present homeowners with ways to avoid foreclosure. Websites which can connect individual borrowers and homeowners to lenders are increasingly offered as mechanisms to bypass traditional lenders while meeting payment obligations for mortgage providers. Although there are slight differences between the states, the foreclosure process generally follows a timeline beginning with initial missed payments, moving to a sale being scheduled and finally a redemption period.

Foreclosure Auction

When the entity (in the US, typically a county sheriff or designee) auctions a foreclosed property the noteholder may set the starting price as the remaining balance on the mortgage loan. However, there are a number of issues that affect how pricing for properties is considered, including bankruptcy rulings. In a weak market the foreclosing party may set the starting price at a lower amount if it believes the real estate securing the loan is worth less than the remaining principal of the loan. Time from notice of foreclosures to actual property sales is dependent on many factors, such as the method of foreclosure (judicial or non-judicial).

In the case where the remaining mortgage balance is higher than the actual home value, the foreclosing party is unlikely to attract auction bids at this price level. A house that has gone through a foreclosure auction and failed to attract any acceptable bids may remain the property of the owner of the mortgage. That inventory is called REO (real estate owned). In these situations the owner/servicer tries to sell it through standard real estate channels.

FLORIDA REAL ESTATE

Chapter 2
Getting Started in Business Step by Step

Getting Started in Business

There are about thirty eight million home-based businesses in the United States alone.

Many people dream of the indepence and financial reward of having a home business. Unfortunately they let analysis paralysis stop them from taking action. This chapter is designed to give you a road map to get started. The most difficult step in any journey is the first step.

Anthony Robbins created a program called Personal Power. I studied the program a long time ago, and today I would summarize it, by saying you must figure out a way to motivate yourself to take massive action without fear of failure.

2 Timothy 1:7 King James Version

"For God hath not given us the spirit of fear; but of power, and of love, and of a sound mind."

Getting Started in Business

STEP #1 MAKE AN OFFICE IN YOUR HOUSE

If you are serious about making money, then redo the man cave or the woman's cave and make a place for you to do business, uninterupted.

STEP #2 BUDGET OUT TIME FOR YOU BUSINESS

If you already have a job, or if you have children, then they can take up a great deal of your time. Not to mention well meaning friends who use the phone to become time theifs. Budget time for your business and stick to it.

STEP #3 DECIDE ON THE TYPE OF BUSINESS

You don't have to be rigid, but begin with the end in mine. You can become more flexible as you gain experience.

Getting Started in Business

STEP #4 LEGAL FORM FOR YOUR BUSINESS

The three basic legal forms are sole proprietorship, partnership, and corporation. Each one has it's advantages. Go to www.Sba.gov and learn about each and make a decision.

STEP #5 PICK A BUSINESS NAME AND REGISTER IT

One of the safest ways to pick a business name is to use your own name. Your own name is not copywrited.

However, always check with an Attorney or the proper legal authority when dealing with legal matters.

Getting Started in Business

STEP #6 WRITE A BUSINESS PLAN

This would seem like a no brainer. No matter what you are trying to accomplish you should have a bluepring. You should have a business plan. In the NFL about seven headcoaches get fired every season. So in a very competetive business, a man with no head coaching experience got hired by the NFL's Philadelphia Eagles. His name was Andy Reid. Andy Reid would later become the most successful coach in the team's history. One of the reasons the owner hired him, was because he had a business plan the size of a telephone book. Your business plan does not need to be nearly that big, but if you plan for as much as possible, you are less likely to get rattled when things don't go as planned.

STEP #7 PROPER LICENSES & PERMITS

Go to city hall and find out what you need to do, to start a home business.

Getting Started in Business

STEP #8 SELECT BUSINESS CARDS, STATIONERY, BROCHURES

This is one of the least expensive ways to not only start your business but to promote and network your business.

STEP #9 OPEN A BUSINESS CHECKING ACCOUNT

Having a separate business account makes it much easier to keep track of profit and expenses. This will come in very handy, whether you decide to do your own taxes or hire out an professional.

STEP #10 TAKE SOME SORT OF ACTION TODAY!

This is not meant to be a comprehensive plan to start a business. It is meant to point you in the right direction to get started. You can go to the Small Business Administration for many free resources for starting your business. They even have a program(SCORE) that will give you access to many retired professionals who will advise you for free! www.score.org

FLORIDA REAL ESTATE

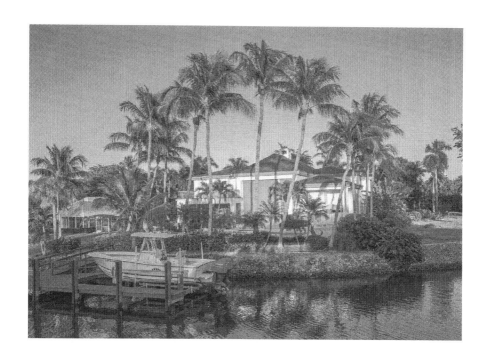

Chapter 3

Small Business Grants

How to write a Winning Grant Proposal

Small Business Grants

Government grants. Many people either don't believe government grants exist or they don't think they would ever be able to get government grant money.

First lets make one thing clear. Government grant money is **YOUR MONEY**. Government money comes from taxes paid by residents of this country. Depending on what state you live in, you are paying taxes on almost everything....Property tax for your house. Property tax on your car. Taxes on the things you purchase in the mall, or at the gas station. Taxes on your gasoline, the food you buy etc.

So get yourself in the frame of mind that you are not a charity case or too proud to ask for help, because billionaire companies like GM, Big Banks and most of Corporate America is not hesitating to get their share of **YOUR MONEY**!

There are over two thousand three hundred (2,300) Federal Government Assistance Programs. Some are loans but many are formula grants and project grants. To see all of the programs available go to:

http://www.CFDA.gov

WRITING A GRANT PROPOSAL

The Basic Components of a Proposal

There are eight basic components to creating a solid proposal package:

1. The proposal summary;

2. Introduction of organization;

3. The problem statement   (or needs assessment);

4. Project objectives;

5. Project methods or design;

6. Project evaluation;

7. Future funding; and

8. The project budget.

The Proposal Summary

The Proposal Summary is an outline of the project goals and objectives. Keep the Proposal Summary short and to the point. No more that 2 or 3 paragraphs. Put it at the beginning the proposal.

Introduction

The Introduction portion of your grant proposal presents you and your business as a credible applicant and organization.

Highlight the accomplishments of your organization from all sources: newspaper or online articles etc. Include a biography of key members and leaders. State the goals and philosophy of the company.

The Problem Statement

The problem statement makes clear the problem you are going to solve(maybe reduce homelessness). Make sure to use facts. State who and how those affected will benefits from solving the problem. State the exact manner in how you will solve the problem.

Project Objectives

The Project Objectives section of your grant proposal focuses on the Goals and Desired outcome.

Make sure to indentify all objectives and how you are going to reach these objectives. The more statistics you can find to support your objectives the better. Make sure to put in realistic objectives. You may be judged on how well you accomplish what you said you intended to do.

Program Methods and Design

The program methods and design section of your grant proposal is a detailed plan of action.

What resources are going to be used.

What staff in going to be needed.

System development

Create a Flow Chart of project features.

Explain what will be achieved.

Try to produce evidence of what will be achieved.

Make a diagram of program design.

Evaluation

There is product evaluation and process evaluation. The product evaluation deals with the result that relate to the project and how well the project has met it's objectives.

The process evaluation deals with how the project was conducted, how did it line up the original stated plan and the overall effectiveness of the different aspects of the plan.

Evaluations can start at anytime during the project or at the project's conclusion. It is advised to submit a evaluation design at the start of a project.

It looks better if you have collected convincing data before and during the program.

If evaluation design is not presented at the beginning that might encourage a critical review of the program design.

Future Funding

The Future Funding part of the grant proposal should have long term project planning past the grant period.

Budget

Utilities, rental equipment, staffing, salary, food, transportation, phone bills and insurance are just some of the things to include in the budget.

A well constructed budget accounts for every penny.

A complete guide for government grants is available at the website link below.

https://www.cfda.gov/downloads/CFDA.GOV_Public_User_Guide_v2.0.pdf

The guide can also be accessed at the very bottom of every page of the https://www.cfda.gov/ website.

Other sources of Government Funding

You can get General Small Business loans from the government. Go to the Small Business Administration for more information.

SBA Microloan Program

The Microloan program provides loans of up to $50,000 with the average loan being $13,000.

https://www.sba.gov/

Chapter 4

Finding Real Estate in Florida

Quick & Easy Access to Foreclosure Real Estate

When Investing in Florida first you have to determine what county you want to purchase in. To help you decide below is a list of all 67 counties in Florida with their population and square miles. After the list of all the counties, you get a Goldmine Rolodex of web site address of Wholesale Government Tax Sale Properties and More!

Florida Counties	Population	Square Miles
1. Miami-Dade County	2,662,874	1,946
2. Broward County	1,780,172	1,209
3. Palm Beach County	1,335,187	2,034
4. Hillsborough County	1,267,775	1,051
5. Orange County	1,169,107	908
6. Pinellas County	917,398	280
7. Duval County	870,709	774

Florida Counties	Population	Square Miles
8. Lee County	631,330	804
9. Polk County	609,492	1,875
10. Brevard County	543,566	1,018
11. Volusia County	494,804	1,106
12. Pasco County	466,457	745
13. Seminole County	425,071	308
14. Sarasota County	382,213	572
15. Marion County	332,529	1,579
16. Collier County	328,134	2,026
17. Manatee County	327,142	741

Florida Counties	Population	Square Miles
18. Lake County	301,019	953
19. Escambia County	299,114	664
20. St. Lucie County	280,379	572
21. Leon County	277,971	667
22. Osceola County	276,163	1,322
23. Alachua County	249,365	874
24. St. Johns County	195,823	609
25. Clay County	192,370	601
26. Okaloosa County	183,482	936
27. Hernando County	173,094	478

Florida Counties	Population	Square Miles
28. Bay County	169,856	764
29. Charlotte County	160,511	694
30. Santa Rosa County	154,104	1,016
31. Martin County	147,495	556
32. Citrus County	140,031	584
33. Indian River County	138,894	503
34. Highlands County	98,630	1,028
35. Sumter County	97,756	546
36. Flagler County	97,376	485
37. Nassau County	74,195	652

Florida Counties	Population	Square Miles
38. Putnam County	74,041	722
39. Monroe County	73,873	997
40. Columbia County	67,485	797
41. Walton County	55,793	1,058
42. Jackson County	49,292	916
43. Gadsden County	46,151	516
44. Suwannee County	41,972	688
45. Levy County	40,156	1,118
46. Okeechobee County	40,140	774
47. Hendry County	39,089	1,153

Florida Counties	Population	Square Miles
48. DeSoto County	34,894	637
49. Wakulla County	30,978	607
50. Bradford County	28,255	293
51. Hardee County	27,887	637
52. Baker County	27,154	585
53. Washington County	24,935	580
54. Taylor County	22,691	1,042
55. Holmes County	19,873	482
56. Madison County	19,115	692
57. Gilchrist County	17,004	349

Florida Counties	Population	Square Miles
58. Dixie County	16,486	704
59. Gulf County	15,844	565
60. Union County	15,388	240
61. Calhoun County	14,750	567
62. Hamilton County	14,671	515
63. Jefferson County	14,658	598
64. Glades County	12,635	774
65. Franklin County	11,596	534
66. Lafayette County	8,942	543
67. Liberty County	8,314	836

FLORIDA

As of the writting of this book, all of these websites are up and running. From time to time some will change their address. If a site does not come up sometimes using the root of the address works. For example if www.mystate.gov/wholesaleproperty does not work. Just go with www.mystate.gov/

FLORIDA TAX SALE PROPERTIES

Broward County:

http://goo.gl/Ed8G7p

Palm Beach County:

http://www.pbcgov.com/papa/

https://mypalmbeachclerk.clerkauction.com/

Seminole County:

http://www.seminoletax.org/

http://www.seminoleclerk.org/TaxDeedSales/

Locate Statewide Florida Properties

MLS

http://www.mls.com/search/florida.mvc

Florida Real Estate Foreclosures with links to different cities on the landing page.

REALTOR

http://www.realtor.com/foreclosures/Florida

Links to Florida real estate properties by county and city.

UNITED STATES REAL ESTATE INFO

http://www.statelocalgov.net/50states-tax-authorities.cfm

http://www.brbpub.com/free-public-records/

www.RealAuction.com

www.GrantStreet.com

Locate Nationwide Foreclosure Auction Properties

http://www.bid4assets.com/

Bid4assets is an amazing website for quickly finding investment property. The landing page has a map of the United States and you can just move your mouse pointer over the state you are interested in to see if they have any property in their database.

Here are just a few of assets you can target on this site!

* County Tax Sales

* Bank Owned Property

* US Marshal

* Real Estate

* Coins

* $1 No Reserve Homes

Locate Nationwide Foreclosure Auction Properties

Http://www.realauction.com

Real Auction is another great website for instant access to property information.

Once on the landing page click "client sites".

They have 4 categories of information.

* Tax Liens Auctions

* Tax Deeds Applications

* Foreclosure and Tax Deed Auctions

* Tax Deed Management

Then chose from the states and counties that appear, that they have auction information.

FLORIDA REAL ESTATE

CHAPTER 5

FINANCING REAL ESTATE

8 Realistic Ways to Finance Real Estate

FINANCING REAL ESTATE

Welcome to Expert financing. I am going to show you several realistic ways to finance real estate. You are going to learn how to finance real estate with.

* VA LOANS

* PARTNERS

* INVESTMENT CLUBS

* CREDIT CARDS

* CORPORATE CREDIT

* EQUITY

* SELLER FINANCE

* HARD MONEY LENDERS

* AND FINALLY I SHOW YOU THE MONEY$!!

USING A VA LOAN

According to the web sites www.benefits.va.gov and www.military.com the current VA Loan amount is a whopping $417,000! What a lot of veterans don't know is that you can use that money to purchase not only your home, but investment properties. That is how I started my investing career. Purchasing multiple homes using my VA Loan.

FINANCING REAL ESTATE

Even if you are not a veteran, you can still partner up with one, who still has some money left on his or her VA LOAN.

If you are a Veteran, you will need to obtain a copy of your DD 214 and VA Form 26-1880 Request for a Certificate of Eligibility.

PARTNERS

This is another way I purchased a home. At the time I worked for the United States Postal Service. I had already purchased plenty of homes, so many of the workers were aware I had successfully invested in real estate. At break time I went around and ask people to partner up with me. I had multiple people offer to go in as a partner. I choose one and that house we rehabbed and flipped just two months after purchasing it. To this day it was the biggest gross profit on one deal, I have had. True I had to split it with my partner, but I would rather have half of something than all of nothing.

Having the combined resources of two people can be a great benefit, but it is not without it's challenges. If you are going to use a partner, no matter how close you are...GET EVERY THING IN WRITING.

FINANCING REAL ESTATE

Having a partner can dramatically increase the chance of a Bank lending moey as well as having someone to split the work on rehabbing, should you decide to save money and make repairs yourself. But all this must be spelled out BEFORE you enter into a Agreement/Contract and purchase a home.

It helps if the person is like minded and understands the risks and benefits of investing, and truly understands the return on investment of a particular deal.

REAL ESTATE INVESTMENT CLUBS

Real estate investment clubs are groups that meet locally and allow investors and other professionals to network and learn. They can provide extremely useful information for both the novice and expert real estate investor. A top real estate club can provide a great forum to network, learn about reputable contractors, brokers, realtors, lawyers, accountants and other professionals. On the other hand, there are many real estate clubs designed to sell you. They bring in "gurus" who sell either on stage or at the back of the room, and as a result, the clubs typically profit to the tune of %50 of the sale price of the product, bootcamp, or training that is pitched.

FINANCING REAL ESTATE

I have purchased a ton of real estate books and real estate courses. Carlton Sheets, Dave Del Dotto, The Mylands, Seminar courses and much much more. I am not against any club bringing in a speaker who has a course. However I think there should be transparency to the members of the club.

There is certainly value in the networking that may come at one of these groups. But attend working to attain your goals and not necessary the a club's goal to sell you something. Some times both are the same thing. As a rule I usually leave debit cards at home the first time I attend an event. If there is a seller there with a "This day only offer" then I won't feel pressured to purchase. Plus most sellers can be convinced to sell at the offer price at a later time when you have had a chance to come down off the "sense of urgency emotional pitch" that many make.

CREDIT CARDS

When using a credit card in real estate you must really do your homework on the deal. Dan Kennedy a world famous marketer once said "always stack the numbers in your favor". That's how you use a credit card. Look at the return on investment as compared to the long term cost of using a credit card and it's interest. Also I would recommend buying low cost homes that you can purchase and own free and clear.

FINANCING REAL ESTATE

No Mortgage Payment!!! My last 2 homes I have purchased have been cash deals. One home cost $1,500 and the other about $7,000. The first was a government property from HUD and the 2nd From a Bank. These institutions are unemotional about real estate and simply view a property as a non performing asset. The 2nd home was 4 bedrooms, 1 1/2 bath and a basement located in a farming community and came with a 2 car garage/shed and .6 acre(that is the size of a NFL football field) of land.

Later in this book I will show you how to find plenty of houses with amazing below wholesale prices and a formula for almost always finding a great deal.

CORPORATE CREDIT

Many people set up corporations to buy and sell real estate as an additional protection against liabilities. Other's create a corporation to mask personal involvement in property transfers and public records. Regardless of the use of a corporation, you can buy real estate with corporate credit as an alternative to using your own cash or IRA. By capitalizing on the credit rating of your corporation, you can buy real estate and build your corporate holdings portfolio.

FINANCING REAL ESTATE

Just remember that you can set up your corporation in a state that favors you the most for your real estate deals. Do your research. Most people like Delaware and Nevada, but you will have to decide if your home state or any other state is best for you and your business.

CURRENT EQUITY

Using the equity in your home for real estate investing is another way you can finance properties. You might use the money for a down payment or it may only be enough to cover the cost of some rehab repairs.

If you stick to the low cost home formula, you may have enough to purchase the entire house. A house is an investment that should appreciate in value as well as give a great ROI (Return On Investment). Whether you decide to flip the property or rent it out for positive cashflow.

If you have equity and it's not doing anything, then you may decide to make it a "performing asset" and use it as part of your real estate finance program.

FINANCING REAL ESTATE

SELLER FINANCING

Seller finance is where the seller of a free and clear property becomes your bank along with being the seller.

Advantages:

You get to purchase the property on terms that may be more beneficial for you. Seller gets monthly payments and the benefit of treating the sale as an installment sale thus allowing them to defer any capital gains taxes that may be due.

Disadvantages:

You may be locked into a mortgage with a pre-payment penalty or may not be able to resell the property immediately. This strategy is typically not meant for flipping but can definitely be used for that purpose if structured correctly.

Because it is a known way to finance a property I have presented it in this book. But it is my least favorite because you now have a lingering relationship with your property. Your ability to make decisions regarding the property is limited and for that reason, I would don't go this route. However, like all types of financing, you have to ask yourself, "is the deal worth it."

FINANCING REAL ESTATE

I also prefer to work alone, but when a great deal came along, I sought out a partner to make it happen. Risk is usually relative to potential profit.

HARD MONEY LENDERS

A hard money lender is usually a individual or company that lends money for investment of a secured by the investment property.

Advantages:

Less red tape the get the money. You are dealing with people who understand the real estate investment business.

Disadvantage:

This is not a long term loan. The lender wants a return on investment, usually within a few months, a a year, or a few years. The interest rate on the loan is much higher than usual conventional banks.

Using hard money has a higher risk because the return on investment is due quicker. Therefore it is good idea not to use a Hard Money Lender, until you have a great deal of experience and confidence in being able to produce a return on investment.

SHOWING YOU THE MONEY

www.businessfinance.com (4,000 sources of money!)

www.advanceamericaproperty.com

http://www.cashadvanceloan.com/

www.brookviewfinancial.com

www.commercialfundingcorp.com

www.dhlc.com
(hard money for the Texas area)

www.equity-funding.com

www.bankofamerica.com

www.carolinahardmoney.com
(for real estate investors in North and South Carolina)

www.fpfloans.com

FLORIDA REAL ESTATE

CHAPTER 6

How to Sell Your House Fast!

12 Steps to Selling Any Property Fast!

How to Sell Your House Fast!

12 Steps to Selling Any Property Fast!

1. Clean and Paint the house

Make sure the house is clean and uncluttered. This makes it easier for buyer to envision themselves living there. Make the bathrooms and kitchen a priority.

2. Scent the house

You might use a light incense or place some vanilla extract and place it on a old school lightbulb to give it a fresh baked cookie smell.

3. Write a property description

Writing a great property description is key to getting buyers interested in your home. One short cut to learning how to write a good property description is to view property listings of sold properties.

4. Take Good pictures

If you don't have a good camera, buy one. A picture is worth a 1,000 words.

How to Sell Your House Fast!

12 Steps to Selling Any Property Fast!

5. Send a email to your buyers list

If you do not have a buyer's list, here is a link to a complete set of training videos on how to build a valuable customer list.

https://goo.gl/UFSIY6

6. Post ads on craigslist

Keep reposting your ads on a daily basis so that you stay at the top of the search results.

7. Post ads to http://www.backpage.com/

This is a Worldwide Classified Ad Web Site.

How to Sell Your House Fast!

12 Steps to Selling Any Property Fast!

8. **Place a Ad on http://realeflow.com/**

This is the number one source for real estate investing leads.

9. **https://www.zillow.com/rental-manager/**

This is a free rental web site.

10. Create a video virtual tour

Create a video virtual tour and upload the video to YouTube. This is a powerful tool. YouTube is 2nd only to Google as the largest Search Engine in the world. However just posting a video won't get it seen. It has to be Search Engine Optimized(SEO). Below is a link to training videos that will show you step by step how to create great videos and get massive traffic viewing them!

https://goo.gl/UFSIY6

How to Sell Your House Fast!

12 Steps to Selling Any Property Fast!

11. Post an ad on facebook target a city

You can place an ad on Facebook and target the city that your property is in.

12. Place a Standard For Sale sign in the yard

If posible have flyers available as well.

13. Place addition white signs in the yard

Give more information and get more attention by placing more personal signs in the yard.

14. List property in the MLS

If you are not a real estate agent get one to do it for you.

How to Sell Your House Fast!

12 Steps to Selling Any Property Fast!

15. Place directional signs

Help people find your house. Make sure you are not violating any county codes when placing signs.

16. Continue marketing until closing

Don't slack off. If necessary you might want to hire VA's Virtual Assistants to keep all ads running.

17. Eliminating Negative Cash Flow

https://www.airbnb.com/

Airbnb is a web site that markets your house or rooms in your house for rent. It's easier to sell your house when it is clean, empty and buyers can envision themselves living in it.

However, if you are suffering from negative cash flow you might want to look into just renting out 1 room in the house.

How to Sell Your House Fast!

12 Steps to Selling Any Property Fast!

18. ZERO COST MARKETING

Below are a few steps to market anything using ZERO COST INTERNET MARKETING STRATEGIES.

While there are many ways to market. In this section we are only going focus on ZERO COST MARKETING. When you are more established you can always go for the more expensive ways of marketing after your business is producing income.

FREE WEB HOSTING

Get a free web site. You can get a free web site at weebly.com or wix.com. Or just type "free web hosting" in a google, bing or yahoo search engine.

Free web hosting is something you can use for a variety or reasons. However many free web hosting sites add an extension to the name of your web address, and that lets everyone know you are using their services. For this reason you eventually want to scale up once you start making income.

How to Sell Your House Fast!

LOW COST PAID WEB HOSTING

Free is nice, but you when you need to expand your business it is best to go with a paid web hosting service. There are several that give you good value for under $10.00 a month.

19. Low Cost Paid Web Hosting

1. Yahoo small business

2. Intuit.com

3. ipage.com

4. Hostgator.com

5. Godaddy.com

6. Webhosting pad

Yahoo small business allows for unlimited web pages and is probably the best overall value, but they require a years payment up front. Intuit allows for monthly payments.

For free ecommerce on your web site, open up a Paypal account and get the HTML code for payment buttons for free. Then put those buttons on your web site.

How to Sell Your House Fast!

20. More Zero Cost Marketing

Step 1 zero cost internet marketing

Now that your web site is up and running you should register it with at least the top 3 search engines.

 1. Google 2. Bing 3. Yahoo.

Step 2 zero cost internet marketing

Write and submit a press release. Google "free press release sites" for press release sites that will allow you to summit press releases for free. If you do not know how to write a press release go to www.fiverr.com and sub-contract the work out for only $5.00 !!!

Step 3 zero cost internet marketing

Write and submit articles to article marketing web sites like ezinearticles.com.

Step 4 zero cost internet marketing

Create and submit videos to video sharing sites like dailymotion.com or youtube.com. Make sure to include a hyperlink to your website in the description of your videos.

Step 5 zero cost internet marketing

Submit your web site to dmoz.org. This is a huge open directory that many smaller search engines go to get web sites for their database.

FLORIDA REAL ESTATE

CHAPTER 7

Millionaire Rolodex

Get Started Fast with these Business Web Sites

As of the writing of this book all, of the companies below, web site is up and have an active business. From time to time companies go out of business or change their web address. So, instead of just giving you just 1 source I give you plenty to choose from.

https://goo.gl/k6DU9k

hit the link above for an instant download of this book!:

Youtube Channel Passive Income Streams Video Marketing Book:

Build an Audience

with YouTube SEO & Make Money on YouTube

Top 15 Most Popular eBizMBA Rank
Real Estate Websites

Estimated Unique Monthly Visitors

1. **Zillow**   36,000,000

2. **Trulia**   23,000,000

3. **Yahoo! Homes**   20,000,000

4. **Realtor**   18,000,000

5. **Redfin**   6,000,000

6. **Homes**   5,000,000

7. **ApartmentGuide**   2,500,000

Top 15 Most Popular eBizMBA Rank

Real Estate Websites

Estimated Unique Monthly Visitors

8. **Curbed**   2,000,000

9. **ReMax**   1,800,000

10. **HotPads**   1,750,000

11. **ZipRealty**   1,600,000

12. **Apartments**   1,500,000

13. **Rent**   1,400,000

14. **Auction**   1,300,000

15. **ForRent**   1,200,000

Nationwide Banks & Foreclosure Properties

Bank of America

http://foreclosures.bankofamerica.com/

Wells Fargo

https://reo.wellsfargo.com/

Ocwen Financial Corporation

http://www.ocwen.com/reo

Hubzu

http://www.hubzu.com/

Government Foreclosure Properties

Fannie Mae
The Federal National Mortgage Association

https://www.fanniemae.com/singlefamily/reo-vendors

Department of Housing and Urban Development

https://www.hudhomestore.com/Home/Index.aspx

The Federal Deposit Insurance Corporation

https://www.fdic.gov/buying/owned/

The **United States Department of Agriculture**

https://properties.sc.egov.usda.gov/resales/index.jsp

United States Marshals

https://www.usmarshals.gov/assets/sales.htm#real_estate

Commercial Real Estate Properties

City Feet

http://www.cityfeet.com/#

The Commercial Real Estate Listing Service

https://www.cimls.com/

Land . Net

http://www.land.net/

Loop . Net

http://www.loopnet.com/

FSBO – For Sale By Owner

By Owner

http://www.byowner.com/

For sale by owner in Canada

http://www.fsbo-bc.com/

For sale by owner Central

http://www.fsbocentral.com/

For sale by Owner: world's largest FSBO web site

http://www.forsalebyowner.com/

Ranch by owner

http://www.ranchbyowner.com/

Tools to Get You Started Video Marketing

https://www.youtube.com/

https://www.wikipedia.org/

https://screencast-o-matic.com/

http://www.openoffice.org/download/

Free Keyword Tools

https://adwords.google.com/home/tools/keyword-planner/

http://www.seocentro.com/

https://ubersuggest.io/

Promoting Your Real Estate/Videos

Top Free Press Release Websites

https://www.prlog.org

https://www.pr.com

https://www.pr-inside.com

https://www.newswire.com

https://www.OnlinePRNews.com

Social Media Websites

https://www.facebook.com

https://www.tumbler.com

https://www.pinterest.com

https://www.reddit.com

https://www.linkedin.com/

http://digg.com/

https://twitter.com

https://plus.google.com/

For Everything Under the Sun at Wholesale

http://www.liquidation.com/

COMPUTERS/Office Equipment

http://www.wtsmedia.com/

http://www.laptopplaza.com/

http://www.outletpc.com/

Computer Tool Kits

http://www.dhgate.com/wholesale/computer+repair+tools.html

http://www.aliexpress.com/wholesale/wholesale-repair-computer-tool.html

http://wholesalecomputercables.com/Computer-Repair-Tool-Kit/M/B00006OXGZ.htm

http://www.tigerdirect.com/applications/category/category_tlc.asp?CatId=47&name=Computer%20Tools

Computer Parts

http://www.laptopuniverse.com/

http://www.sabcal.com/

other

http://www.nearbyexpress.com/

http://www.commercialbargains.co

http://www.getpaid2workfromhome.com

http://www.boyerblog.com/success-tools

Small Business Resources

1.   http://www.sba.gov/content/starting-green-business

2.   http://www.sba.gov/content/home-based-business

3.   online businesses

http://www.sba.gov/content/setting-online-business

4.   self employed and independent contractors

http://www.sba.gov/content/self-employed-independent-contractors

5.   minority owned businesses

http://www.sba.gov/content/minority-owned-businesses

6.   veteran owned businesses

http://www.sba.gov/content/veteran-service-disabled-veteran-owned

7.   woman owned businesses

http://www.sba.gov/content/women-owned-businesses

8.   people with disabilities

http://www.sba.gov/content/people-with-disabilities

9.   young entrepreneurs

http://www.sba.gov/content/young-entrepreneurs

CHAPTER 8

REAL ESTATE TERMS

REAL ESTATE TERMS

Acceleration Clause - A contract provision that allows a lender to require a borrower to repay all or part of an outstanding loan if certain requirements are not met. An acceleration clause outlines the reasons that the lender can demand loan repayment. Also known as "acceleration covenant".

Accrued Depreciation - Depreciation is the loss in value to any structure due to a variety of factors, such as wear and tear, age, and poor location. The term accrued depreciation means the total depreciation of a building from all causes.

Accrued Interest - In finance, accrued interest is the interest on a bond or loan that has accumulated since the principal investment, or since the previous coupon payment if there has been one already. For a financial instrument such as a bond, interest is calculated and paid in set intervals (for instance annually or semi-annually).

Active Income - Active income is income for which services have been performed. This includes wages, tips, salaries, commissions and income from businesses in which there is material participation.

REAL ESTATE TERMS

Add-on Interest - A method of calculating interest whereby the interest payable is determined at the beginning of a loan and added onto the principal. The sum of the interest and principal is the amount repayable upon maturity.

Adjustable Rate Mortgage (ARM) - A variable-rate mortgage, adjustable-rate mortgage (ARM), or tracker mortgage is a mortgage loan with the interest rate on the note periodically adjusted based on an index which reflects the cost to the lender of borrowing on the credit markets.

Cash flow after taxes (CFAT) - Cash flow after taxes (CFAT) is a measure of financial performance that looks at the company's ability to generate cash flow through its operations. It is calculated by adding back non-cash accounts such as amortization, depreciation, restructuring costs and impairments to net income.

Agent - One who is legally authorized to act on behalf of another person.

Agreement for sale - An agreement of sale constitutes the terms and conditions of sale of a property by the seller to the buyer. ... Sale deed is the document prepared at the time of full payment made by the buyer and when the actual transfer of the property takes place.

REAL ESTATE TERMS

Alienation clause - A clause in a mortgage contract that requires full payment of the balance of a mortgage at the lender's discretion if the property is sold or the title to the property changes to another person. Nearly all mortgages have an alienation clause.

All-inclusive deed of trust (AITD) - An All Inclusive Trust Deed (AITD) is a new deed of trust that includes the balance due on the existing note plus new funds advanced; also known as a wrap-around mortgage.

American Land Title Association (ALTA) -The American Land Title Association (ALTA) is a trade association representing the title insurance industry. Founded in 1907, ALTA also focuses on a property's abstract of title, which ties the history of the title to a particular piece of real estate.

Amortization - Amortization is an accounting term that refers to the process of allocating the cost of an intangible asset over a period of time. It also refers to the repayment of loan principal over time.

Amortized loan - An amortized loan is a loan with scheduled periodic payments that consist of both principal and interest. An amortized loan payment pays the relevant interest expense for the period before any principal is paid and reduced.

REAL ESTATE TERMS

Appraisal - an expert estimate of the value of something.

Appraised value - An appraised value is an evaluation of a property's value based on a given point in time that is performed by a professional appraiser during the mortgage origination process. The appraiser is usually chosen by the lender, but the appraisal is paid for by the borrower.

Appraiser - A practitioner who has the knowledge and expertise necessary to estimate the value of an asset, or the likelihood of an event occurring, and the cost of such an occurrence.

Arbitration - the use of an arbitrator to settle a dispute.

Arbitration clause - An arbitration clause is a clause in a contract that requires the parties to resolve their disputes through an arbitration process

Asking price - the price at which something is offered for sale.

Assessment - the evaluation or estimation of the nature, quality, or ability of someone or something.

Assignee - a person to whom a right or liability is legally transferred.

REAL ESTATE TERMS

Assignment - An assignment (Latin cessio) is a term used with similar meanings in the law of contracts and in the law of real estate. In both instances, it encompasses the transfer of rights held by one party—the assignor—to another party—the assignee.

Assumption Clause - A provision in a mortgage contract that allows the seller of a home to pass responsibility to the buyer of the home for the existing mortgage. In other words, the new homeowner assumes the existing mortgage. There are typically many conditions and a fee required in an assumption clause.

Assumption of mortgage - Mortgage assumption is the conveyance of the terms and balance of an existing mortgage to the purchaser of a financed property, commonly requiring that the assuming party is qualified under lender or guarantor guidelines.

At-risk rule - Tax laws limiting the amount of losses an investor (usually a limited partner) can claim. Only the amount actually at risk can be deducted.

REAL ESTATE TERMS

Authorization to sell - Authorization to sell is a listing contract whereby a representative is employed by a seller to secure a buyer for the property. An authorization to sell does not give the agent the authority to enter into a binding contract of sale.

Backup offer - A backup offer is when a home seller has accepted an offer from a buyer, but is still accepting offers from other buyers. Sellers state that they are accepting backup offers if they think the current offer may fall through

Balloon mortgage - a mortgage in which a large portion of the borrowed principal is repaid in a single payment at the end of the loan period.

Balloon payment - a repayment of the outstanding principal sum made at the end of a loan period, interest only having been paid hitherto.

Binder insurance - binder. A legal agreement issued by either an agent or an insurer to provide temporary evidence of insurance until a policy can be issued. Binders should contain definite time limits, should be in writing, and should clearly designate the insurer with which the risk is bound

Capital gain - a profit from the sale of property or of an investment.

REAL ESTATE TERMS

Capitalization - the provision of capital for a company, or the conversion of income or assets into capita

Cash basis taxpayer - A taxpayer who reports income and deductions in the year that they are actually paid or received. Cash basis taxpayers cannot report receivables as income, nor deduct promissory notes as payments.

Cash flow - the total amount of money being transferred into and out of a business, especially as affecting liquidity.

Certificate of title - A certificate of title is a state or municipal-issued document that identifies the owner or owners of personal or real property. A certificate of title provides documentary evidence of the right of ownership.

Chattel - an item of property other than real estate.

Closing costs - Closing costs are fees paid at the closing of a real estate transaction. This point in time called the closing is when the title to the property is conveyed (transferred) to the buyer. Closing costs are incurred by either the buyer or the seller.

REAL ESTATE TERMS

Cloud on title - Any document, claim, unreleased lien or encumbrance that might invalidate or impair the title to real property or make the title doubtful. Clouds on title are usually discovered during a title search. Clouds on title are resolved through initiating a quitclaim deed or a commencement of action to quiet title.

Co-insurance - a type of insurance in which the insured pays a share of the payment made against a claim.

Collateral - something pledged as security for repayment of a loan, to be forfeited in the event of a default.

Commission - A fee charged by a broker or agent for his/her service in facilitating a transaction, such as the buying or selling of securities or real estate. In the case of securities trading, brokers can be split into two broad categories depending on the commissions they charge.

Contract of sale - A real estate contract is a contract between parties for the purchase and sale, exchange, or other conveyance of real estate.

REAL ESTATE TERMS

Cost approach - Cost approach. ... The fundamental premise of the cost approach is that a potential user of real estate won't, or shouldn't, pay more for a property than it would cost to build an equivalent. The cost of construction minus depreciation, plus land, therefore is a limit, or at least a metric, of market value.

Debt coverage ratio - In corporate finance, DSCR refers to the amount of cash flow available to meet annual interest and principal payments on debt, including sinking fund payments. In personal finance, DSCR refers to a ratio used by bank loan officers in determining debt servicing ability.

Declining balance method - A declining balance method is a common depreciation-calculation system that involves applying the depreciation rate against the non-depreciated balance.

Deed - A deed (anciently "an evidence") is any legal instrument in writing which passes, affirms or confirms an interest, right, or property and that is signed, attested, delivered, and in some jurisdictions, sealed. It is commonly associated with transferring (conveyancing) title to property.

REAL ESTATE TERMS

Deed of trust - In real estate in the United States, a deed of trust or trust deed is a deed wherein legal title in real property is transferred to a trustee, which holds it as security for a loan (debt) between a borrower and lender. The equitable title remains with the borrower.

Depreciation - Depreciation is an accounting method of allocating the cost of a tangible asset over its useful life. Businesses depreciate long-term assets for both tax and accounting purposes.

Double escrow - Double escrow. ... Double escrow is a set of real estate transactions involving two contracts of sale for the same property, to two different back-to-back buyers, at the same or two different prices, arranged to close on the same day.

Due diligence - Due diligence means taking caution, performing calculations, reviewing documents, procuring insurance, walking the property, etc. — essentially doing your homework for the property BEFORE you actually make the purchase

REAL ESTATE TERMS

Earnest money - Earnest money is a deposit made to a seller showing the buyer's good faith in a transaction. Often used in real estate transactions, earnest money allows the buyer additional time when seeking financing. Earnest money is typically held jointly by the seller and buyer in a trust or escrow account.

Eminent domain - Eminent Domain. The power of the government to take private property and convert it into public use. The Fifth Amendment provides that the government may only exercise this power if they provide just compensation to the property owners.

Encroachment - A situation in real estate where a property owner violates the property rights of his neighbor by building something on the neighbor's land or by allowing something to hang over onto the neighbor's property.

Equity participation - Equity participation is the ownership of shares in a company or property. ... The greater the equity participation rate, the higher the percentage of shares owned by stakeholders. Allowing stakeholders to own shares ties the stakeholders' success with that of the company or real estate investment.

REAL ESTATE TERMS

Escrow - Escrow generally refers to money held by a third-party on behalf of transacting parties. ... It is best known in the United States in the context of real estate (specifically in mortgages where the mortgage company establishes an escrow account to pay property tax and insurance during the term of the mortgage).

Escrow instructions - n. the written instructions by buyer and seller of real estate given to a title company, escrow company or individual escrow in "closing" a real estate transaction. These instructions are generally prepared by the escrow holder and then approved by the parties and their agents. (See: closing, escrow)

Estoppel - Estoppel Certificate. An estoppel certificate is a document used in mortgage negotiations to establish facts and financial obligations, such as outstanding amounts due that can affect the settlement of a loan. It is required by a lender of a third party in a real estate transaction

Exclusive right to sell listing - An Exclusive Right to Sell/Lease means that the listing brokerage has an exclusive listing agreement with the Seller. (Sorry about using a word in the term to define the term!) It means that a commission would be owed to the Listing Brokerage when the property is sold to a buyer, regardless of who brings the buyer.

REAL ESTATE TERMS

Fair market value - The fair market value is the price at which the property would change hands between a willing buyer and a willing seller, neither being under any compulsion to buy or to sell and both having reasonable knowledge of relevant facts.

Fee simple - In English law, a fee simple or fee simple absolute is an estate in land, a form of freehold ownership. It is a way that real estate may be owned in common law countries, and is the highest possible ownership interest that can be held in real property.

First right of refusal - A right of first refusal is a contractual right granted by an owner of property. The owner gives the holder of the right an opportunity to enter into a business transaction with the owner according to specified terms, before the owner may enter into that transaction with a third party.

Foreclosure - Foreclosure is a legal process in which a lender attempts to recover the balance of a loan from a borrower, who has stopped making payments to the lender, by forcing the sale of the asset used as the collateral for the loan.

REAL ESTATE TERMS

Gift deed - Quitclaim Deed Vs. Gift Deed. Property deeds define and protect ownership in a home. In real estate, deeds are legal documents that transfer ownership of a property from one party to another. ... Each type of deed is used for a specific situation.

Grantee - In real estate, the grantee is the recipient of a property - the person who will be taking title, as named in the the legal document used to transfer the real estate. The person who is relinquishing the property is called the grantor.

Grantor - First, it's important to review the legal definition of "grantor" and "grantee." In a real estate transaction, the grantor is the party that conveys the property in question. The grantor may be an individual, business entity or partnership. The grantee is the party that receives the property

Gross income - A real estate investment term, Gross Operating Income refers to the result of subtracting the credit and vacancy losses from a property's gross potential income. Also Known As: Effective Gross Income (EGI)

Gross rent multiplier - Gross Rent Multiplier is the ratio of the price of a real estate investment to its annual rental income before accounting for expenses such as property taxes, insurance, utilities, etc.

REAL ESTATE TERMS

Highest and best use - The Appraisal Institute defines highest and best use as follows: The reasonably probable and legal use of vacant land or an improved property that is physically possible, appropriately supported, financially feasible, and that results in the highest value.

Income approach to value - The income approach is a real estate appraisal method that allows investors to estimate the value of a property by taking the net operating income of the rent collected and dividing it by the capitalization rate.

Installment sale - A method of sale that allows for partial deferral of any capital gain to future taxation years. Installment sales require the buyer to make regular payments, or installments, on an annual basis, plus interest if installment payments are to be made in subsequent taxation years.

Insurable title - Marketable Title vs. Insurable Title. ... When a title is marketable it means that the chain of ownership (title) to a particular piece of property is clear and free from defects. And as such, it can be marketed for sale without additional effort by the seller or potential buyer.

REAL ESTATE TERMS

Interest - Estates and ownership interests defined. The law recognizes different sorts of interests, called estates, in real property. The type of estate is generally determined by the language of the deed, lease, bill of sale, will, land grant, etc., through which the estate was acquired.

Internal rate of return (IRR) - Internal rate of return (IRR) is a metric used in capital budgeting measuring the profitability of potential investments. Internal rate of return is a discount rate that makes the net present value (NPV) of all cash flows from a particular project equal to zero. ... r = discount rate, and. t = number of time periods

Involuntary lien - involuntary lien. A lien on real estate that results without the property owners' voluntary cooperation in the placement of the lien. Examples include tax liens and judgment liens. Contrast with a mortgage,which is voluntary.

Joint and several note - Joint and several note is a promissory note which is the note of all and of each of the makers as to its legal obligation between the parties to it.

REAL ESTATE TERMS

Joint tenancy - A type of property right where two or more people own or rent a property together, each with equal rights and obligations, until one owner dies. Upon an owner's death, that owner's interest in the property passes to the survivors without the property having to go through probate.

Judgment proof - People are judgment-proof if they lack the resources or insurance to pay a court judgment against them. For example, suppose that a thief steals your car, sells it, and then burns all of his worldly possessions. Even if you sued him and won, you could not recover anything because the thief is judgment-proof.

Lease option - A lease option (more formally Lease With the Option to Purchase) is a type of contract used in both residential and commercial real estate. In a lease-option, a property owner and tenant agree that, at the end of a specified rental period for a given property, the renter has the option of purchasing the property.

Letter of credit - 1. INTRODUCTION. Letters of credit are often used in real estate transactions to secure obligations. ... For example, a tenant may request its bank to issue a letter of credit to the landlord as security. In such a transaction, the tenant is the applicant, the bank is the issuer and the landlord is the beneficiary.

REAL ESTATE TERMS

Leverage - Leverage is the use of various financial instruments or borrowed capital to increase the potential return of an investment – and it is an extremely common term on both Wall Street and in the Main Street real estate market. (Learn more about the various uses of leverage in Leveraged Investment Showdown.)

Like kind property - Like-Kind Property. Any two assets or properties that are considered to be the same type, making an exchange between them tax free. To qualify as like kind, two assets must be of the same type (e.g. two pieces of residential real estate), but do not have to be of the same quality.

Limited partnership - RELP' A limited partnership entity organized to invest in real estate. A Real Estate Limited Partnership is typically organized with an experienced property manager or real estate development firm serving as the general partner.

Lis pendens - In United States law, a lis pendens is a written notice that a lawsuit has been filed concerning real estate, involving either the title to the property or a claimed ownership interest in it.

REAL ESTATE TERMS

Loan to value - The loan to value or LTV ratio of a property is the percentage of the property's value that is mortgaged. ... Loan to Value is used in commercial real estate as well. Examples: $300,000 appraised value of a home. $240,000 mortgage on the property. $240,000 / $300,000 = .80 or 80% Loan to Value Ratio

Market value - Market value is the most probable price that a property should bring in a competitive and open market under all conditions requisite to a fair sale, the buyer and seller, each acting prudently, knowledgeably and assuming the price is not affected by undue stimulus.

Mechanics lien - A guarantee of payment to builders, contractors and construction firms that build or repair structures. Mechanic's liens also extend to suppliers of materials and subcontractors and cover building repairs as well.

Mortgage broker - A mortgage broker is an intermediary working with a borrower and a lender while qualifying the borrower for a mortgage. The broker gathers income, asset and employment documentation, a credit report and other information for assessing the borrower's ability to secure financing.

REAL ESTATE TERMS

Multiple listing - A multiple listing service (MLS, also multiple listing system or multiple listings service) is a suite of services that real estate brokers use to establish contractual offers of compensation (among brokers) and accumulate and disseminate information to enable appraisals.

Net income - Net operating income (NOI) is a calculation used to analyze real estate investments that generate income. Net operating income equals all revenue from the property minus all reasonably necessary operating expenses

Net rentable area - Actual square-unit of a building that may be leased or rented to tenants, the area upon which the lease or rental payments are computed. It usually excludes common areas, elevator shafts, stairways, and space devoted to cooling, heating, or other equipment. Also called net leasable area.

Non-recourse note - Nonrecourse debt or a nonrecourse loan is a secured loan (debt) that is secured by a pledge of collateral, typically real property, but for which the borrower is not personally liable.

REAL ESTATE TERMS

Obsolescence - Functional obsolescence is a reduction in the usefulness or desirability of an object because of an outdated design feature, usually one that cannot be easily changed. The term is commonly used in real estate, but has a wide application.

Option - A real estate purchase option is a contract on a specific piece of real estate that allows the buyer the exclusive right to purchase the property. Once a buyer has an option to buy a property, the seller cannot sell the property to anyone else.

Passive activity income - Internal Revenue Service (IRS) defines two types of passive activity: trade or business activities not materially participated in, and rental activities even if the taxpayer materially participated in them (unless the taxpayer is a real estate professional).

Point - In real estate mortgages, a point refers to the origination fee charged by the lender, with each point being equal to 1% of the amount of the loan. It can also refer to each percentage difference between a mortgage's interest rate and the prime interest rate.

Possession - A principle of real estate law that allows a person who possesses someone else's land for an extended period of time to claim legal title to that land.

REAL ESTATE TERMS

Potential gross income - The amount of income produced by a piece of property, plus miscellaneous income, less vacancy costs and collection losses. Effective gross income is a metric commonly used to evaluate the value of a piece of investment property. ... The EGI for the property is $500,000 - $100,000, or $400,000.

Preliminary title report - A preliminary title sets forth various details about a piece of real estate, including: Ownership;

   Liens and encumbrances; and Easements.

The information in a preliminary title report, also known as a title search, is gathered from the property records in the county where the property is located.

Prepayment penalty - Prepayment Penalty. A prepayment penalty is a clause in a mortgage contract stating that a penalty will be assessed if the mortgage is prepaid within a certain time period. The penalty is based on a percentage of the remaining mortgage balance or a certain number of months' worth of interest.

Principal - In commercial law, a principal is a person, legal or natural, who authorizes an agent to act to create one or more legal relationships with a third party.

REAL ESTATE TERMS

Pro forma - What does 'Pro Forma' mean. Pro forma, a Latin term, literally means "for the sake of form" or "as a matter of form." In the world of investing, pro forma refers to a method by which financial results are calculated. This method of calculation places emphasis on present or projected figures.

Promissory note - In the United States, a mortgage note (also known as a real estate lien note, borrower's note) is a promissory note secured by a specified mortgage loan; it is a written promise to repay a specified sum of money plus interest at a specified rate and length of time to fulfill the promise.

Property management - Property management is the operation, control, and oversight of real estate as used in its most broad terms. Management indicates a need to be cared for, monitored and accountability given for its useful life and condition.

Quit claim deed - A quitclaim deed is a legal instrument which is used to transfer interest in real property. The entity transferring its interest is called the grantor, and when the quitclaim deed is properly completed and executed, it transfers any interest the grantor has in the property to a recipient, called the grantee.

REAL ESTATE TERMS

Real estate owned (REO) - Real estate owned or REO is a term used in the United States to describe a class of property owned by a lender—typically a bank, government agency, or government loan insurer—after an unsuccessful sale at a foreclosure auction.

Real property - Real estate is "property consisting of land and the buildings on it, along with its natural resources such as crops, minerals or water; immovable property of this nature; an interest vested in this (also) an item of real property, (more generally) buildings or housing in general.

Realized gain - The amount by which the sale price of an asset exceeds its purchase price. Unless the realized gain came from a tax-exempt or tax-deferred asset, it is taxable. However, the type of taxation to which it is subject varies according to how long the asset has been owned. A realized gain from an asset owned longer than one year is usually taxed at the capital gains rate, while an asset owned for a period shorter than a year is often subject to the higher income tax rate. It is also called the recognized gain.

REAL ESTATE TERMS

Refinancing - Getting a new mortgage to replace the original is called refinancing. Refinancing is done to allow a borrower to obtain a better interest term and rate. The first loan is paid off, allowing the second loan to be created, instead of simply making a new mortgage and throwing out the original mortgage.

Rental concession - Rental Concessions are benefits that are offered by the landlord to his tenants. Concessions are usually offered to draw tenants to vacant properties. Some other landlords may choose to offer a concession if the tenant decides to renew the lease. Even when the landlord is planning to sell a home, in return for his tenants co-operation he may offer incentives or concessions.

Replacement cost - A replacement cost is the cost to replace an asset of a company at the same or equal value, and the asset to be replaced could be a building, investment securities, accounts receivable or liens.

Reproduction cost - The costs involved with identically reproducing an asset or property with the same materials and specifications as an insured property based on current prices.

REAL ESTATE TERMS

Rescission - Rescission is the cancellation of a real estate contract between the buyer and seller. The act of rescinding a contract will "unwind" the transaction specified in the contract. A real estate contract may be rescinded at varying points during a transaction.

Restrictive covenant - A restrictive covenant is any type of agreement that requires the buyer to either take or abstain from a specific action. In real estate transactions, restrictive covenants are binding legal obligations written into the deed of a property by the seller.

Right of survivorship - The right of survivorship is an attribute of several types of joint ownership of property, most notably joint tenancy and tenancy in common. When jointly owned property includes a right of survivorship, the surviving owner automatically absorbs a dying owner's share of the property. Thus if A and B jointly own a house with a right of survivorship, and B dies, A becomes the sole owner of the house, despite any contrary intent in B's will.

REAL ESTATE TERMS

Secondary mortgage market - A secondary mortgage market is the market where mortgage loans and servicing rights are bought and sold between mortgage originators, mortgage aggregators (securitizers) and investors. The secondary mortgage market is extremely large and liquid.

Short-rate - The relatively higher insurance premium rate charged for coverage when one cancels a policy earlier than originally agreed upon. Rather than receiving a pro rata refund of the unearned premium,the property owner receives a smaller amount.

Standby commitment - A standby commitment is a formal agreement by a bank agreeing to lend money to a borrower up to a specified amount for a specific period. It is also known as firm commitment lending. The amount given under standby commitment is to be used only in specified contingency.

Subject to mortgage - circumstance in which a buyer takes title to mortgaged real property but is not personally liable for the payment of the amount due. The buyer must make payments in order to keep the property; however, with default, only the buyer's equity in that property is lost. Contrast assumption of mortgage.

REAL ESTATE TERMS

Subordination - For an individual, the most frequent example of a subordination agreement is when an individual attempts to refinance the first mortgage on a property which has a second mortgage. The second mortgage has a lower priority than the first mortgage, but these priorities may be upset by refinancing the loan.

Supply and demand - The law of supply and demand is a basic economic principle that explains the relationship between supply and demand for a good or service and how the interaction affects the price of that good or service. The relationship of supply and demand affects the housing market and the price of a house

Tax lien - A tax lien is a lien imposed by law upon a property to secure the payment of taxes. A tax lien may be imposed for delinquent taxes owed on real property or personal property, or as a result of failure to pay income taxes or other taxes.

Tax shelter -Tax shelters can range from investments or investment accounts that provide favorable tax ... evasion, the illegal avoidance of taxes through misrepresentation or similar means. ... A tax shelter product designed to create large, seemingly real .

REAL ESTATE TERMS

Tenancy by entirety - Tenants by entirety (TBE) is a method in some states by which married couples can hold the title to a property. In order for one spouse to modify his or her interest in the property in any way, the consent of both spouses is required by tenants by entirety.

Tenants-in-common - Tenancy in common is a type of shared ownership of property, where each owner owns a share of the property. Unlike in a joint tenancy, these shares can be of unequal size, and can be freely transferred to other owners both during life and via a will.

Title - a right or claim to the ownership of property or to a rank or throne.

Title insurance policy - Title insurance is an insurance policy that covers the loss of ownership interest in a property due to legal defects and is required if the property is under mortgage. The most common type of title insurance is a lender's title insurance, which is paid for by the borrower but protects only the lender.

Trust deed - a deed of conveyance creating and setting out the conditions of a trust

Usury - the illegal action or practice of lending money at unreasonably high rates of interest.

REAL ESTATE TERMS

Vacancy and rent loss - Vacancy and Credit Loss in real estate investing is the amount of money or percentage of net operating income that is estimated to not be realized due to non-payment of rents and vacant units

Vacancy factor - The vacancy rate is the percentage of all available units in a rental property, such as a hotel or apartment complex, that are vacant or unoccupied at a particular time. It is the opposite of the occupancy rate, which is the percentage of units in a rental property that are occupied.

Warranty deed - a deed that guarantees a clear title to the buyer of real property.

Will - A will or testament is a legal document by which a person, the testator, expresses their wishes as to how their property is to be distributed at death, and names one or more persons, the executor, to manage the estate until its final distribution.

Without recourse - a formula used to disclaim responsibility for future nonpayment, especially of a negotiable financial instrument.

Wrap-around - "wrap", is a form of secondary financing for the purchase of real property. The seller extends to the buyer a junior mortgage which wraps around and exists in addition to any superior mortgages already secured by the property.

FLORIDA REAL ESTATE

Please Leave a Great Review!

I have purchased all of the top real estate investing books on the market, and most have a handful of out dated web sites for their sources of properties.

There is not another real estate investing book on the market that gives you as many sources for wholesale real estate than this book.

My book gives you more and in most cases for less!

This book also gives you a web site that has over 4,000 sources of real estate financing in addition to the government's over 2,400 sources of Federal Assistance.

I have enjoyed doing all the research and sharing my real world real estate investing experience in what I hope is easy to understand terminology.

So I ask you to leave a honest and hopefully great review!

Thank you. Warm Regards,

Brian Mahoney

Join Our VIP Mailing List and Get FREE Money Making Training Videos! Then Start Making Money within 24 hours!
Plus if you join our Mailing list you can get Revised and New Edition versions of your book free!

And Notifications of other FREE Offers!

Just Hit/Type in the Link Below

https://mahoneyproducts.wixsite.com/win1

Get Our Video Training Program at:

**(Zero Cost Internet Marketing
complete 142 video series)
Amazing Training Videos!**

**YouTube Video Marketing
Email Marketing
Copy writing
Set up a Squeeze page
Getting Massive Web Traffic**

https://goo.gl/Qed1dY

Learn how to Get Massive Money
for Real Estate Investing
@

http://www.BrianSMahoney.com

Made in the USA
Monee, IL
13 May 2020

30511716R00067